C000294673

5

Text: David Dunford
Series editor: Tony Bowerman
Photographs: David Dunford, Carl Rogers, Tony Bowerman, Stephen Wagstaff, Shutterstock, Dreamstime, Adobe Stock

Design: Carl Rogers and Laura Hodgkinson

© Northern Eye Books Limited 2020

Ordnance Survey Licensed Mapping — Partner

MIX — Paper from responsible sources
FSC www.fsc.org — FSC® C022174

Northern Eye

A CIP catalogue record for this book is available from the British Library.

www.northerneyebooks.co.uk

Cover: Boot Inn at Willington, near Kelsall (Walk 5)

Important Advice: The routes described in this book are undertaken at the reader's own risk. Walkers should take into account their level of fitness, wear suitable footwear and clothing, and carry food and water. It is also advisable to take the relevant OS map with you in case you get lost and leave the area covered by our maps.

Whilst every care has been taken to ensure the accuracy of the route directions, the publishers cannot accept responsibility for errors or omissions, or for changes in the details given. Nor can the publisher and copyright owners accept responsibility for any consequences arising from the use of this book.

If you find any inaccuracies in either the text or maps, please write or email us at the address below. Thank you.

First published in 2020 by:

Northern Eye Books Limited
Northern Eye Books, Tattenhall, Cheshire CH3 9PX

tony@northerneyebooks.com
www.northerneyebooks.co.uk

  @northerneyebooks

 @northerneyeboo

For sales enquiries, please call 01928 723 744

Printed and bound in the UK by Severn

ISBN 978-1-908632-81-4

Contents

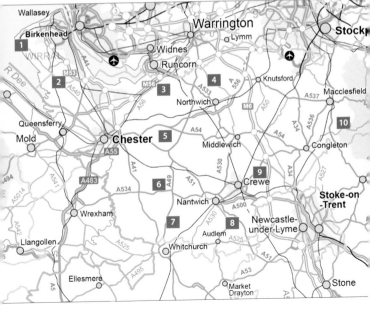

Cheshire and **Wirral**

A POEM OF 1612 BY MICHAEL DRAYTON DESCRIBES, in the florid style of the age, how Cheshire is confined *'twixt two so famous floods as Mersey is and Dee'* and flanked by the *'mountainous and wild'* Peak District.

This handy walking guide explores this *'thrice-happy shire'* and its finest pubs and inns on foot, from the broad rivers and estuaries of the west to the rugged hills of the east, encompassing the valleys of the Weaver and Dee and the wooded mid-Cheshire ridge between them.

Cheshire is unfairly overlooked by walkers in particular and tourists in general, tempted by better-known upland National Parks to the north, east and west, but this obscurity has benefits for the discerning foot traveller. This unassuming and quiet rural landscape, criss-crossed by ancient saltways between attractive villages, has subtle rewards, surprising corners and an undiscovered cachet — a county for the connoisseur, perhaps.

A sunny summer lunchtime outside the White Lion at Barthomley

Cheshire's best pubs and inns

The expectations of the well-heeled Cheshire set have forced the county's hostelries to up their game, to the benefit of visitors. Most of the pubs and inns here manage the delicate balancing act of combining an unpretentious welcome with modern expectations of food, drink and service. Local breweries have sprung up to serve these demanding palates too, and Cheshire's culinary treasures, including its famous cheese, enliven local menus.

As with the landscape, the pubs of Cheshire are diverse: their locations range from estuarine saltmarsh to pretty village and isolated hilltop splendour, but all will satisfy the visitor in search of well-earned sustenance after a hearty stroll.

"And when I was a bruer longe, with hoppes
I made my alle stronge; esshes and hearbes I
blend amonge and marred so good malt."

Chester Mystery Plays (c. 15th century)

TOP 10 Walks: Cheshire's best Pub Walks

AS BEFITS A WEALTHY, FERTILE COUNTY with a rich farming heritage, the country pubs of Cheshire are often a delight. From numerous candidates we've whittled the list down to personal favourites that balance a lack of pretention with great food and drink, and good service. These carefully chosen pubs and inns are also blessed with pleasant locations and rewarding walks from the doorstep, while attempting a representative geographical distribution covering the full range of landscapes of Cheshire and Wirral.

West Kirby Tap
West Kirby

page 8

Harp Inn
Little Neston

page 14

The Ring o' Bells
Frodsham

page 18

George & Dragon
Great Budworth

page 24

The Boot Inn
Kelsall

The Pheasant Inn
Burwardsley

The Swan
Marbury

Swan Inn
Wybunbury

White Lion Inn
Barthomley

The Ship Inn
Wincle

The West Kirby Tap serves a huge range of well-kept real ales

West Kirby Tap
West Kirby

What to expect:
Level paths, beach and dunes, with one short, steep climb at the end

Distance/time: 11 kilometres / 6¾ miles. Allow 3 hours

Start: Free parking on South Parade and adjoining streets, West Kirby

Grid ref: SJ 210 866

Ordnance Survey Map: Explorer Outdoor Leisure 266 *Wirral & Chester/Caer*

The Pub: West Kirby Tap, Grange Road, West Kirby CH48 4DY 0151 625 0350 | www.westkirbytap.co.uk

Walk outline: Leaving West Kirby, the path leads between golf courses to the seafront at Hoylake, then follows the beach to Red Rocks overlooking Hilbre Island. A delightful grassy path continues between dunes and estuary back to West Kirby. The subsequent loop heads around the Marine Lake, follows a short stretch of the Wirral Way, then climbs to views over the Wirral coast, before descending to the start.

Housed in an ordinary building in the centre of town, the West Kirby Tap manages to combine an open-plan tapas-bar buzz with a friendly, shabby-chic pub ambience. Dog-owners, walkers and real-ale aficionados will feel equally welcome in this unpretentious but lively outlet.

Pavement tables

▶ West Kirby Tap at a glance

Open: 12 noon–11pm daily
Brewery/company: Spitting Feathers, Chester
Real ales: Spitting Feathers regulars feature among eight hand-pulled ales, alongside craft beers and speciality gins
Food: Mediterranean- and British-style snacks and sharing platters, served till 9pm. Vegan, vegetarian and gluten-free options available
Accommodation: None
Outside: Café-style pavement tables out front
Children & dogs: Children and dogs very welcome, the former during the day only

Sailing dinghies on the Marine Lake at West Kirby at sunset

The Walk

1. From the **Wirral Sailing Centre** at the northern end of the **Marine Lake**, walk up **Dee Lane** towards the town centre. Pass Morrison's on the right and at the T-junction turn left into **Grange Road**, passing the **West Kirby Tap**.

2. Turn right into **Bridge Road**, passing Aldi on the right. Once over the **railway bridge**, turn left into **Orrysdale Road**. At the end of the road, join the **Wirral Circular Trail cycleway** straight ahead, which bends left then right alongside the railway to **Hoylake Municipal Golf Course**. Five hundred metres after the start of the golf course, turn left onto a public footpath that crosses the railway at a **level crossing** and leads out to the main road. Cross and turn right. After 100 metres, turn left into a public footpath onto the **Royal Liverpool Golf Course**.

3. Turn right along a **tarmac drive** along the edge of the course and then continue across the grass in front of the **clubhouse**. Towards the end of the course, head diagonally left to an exit in the far corner out to **Stanley Road**. Turn right past **St Hildeburgh's Parish**

Church then left at the **Green Lodge Hotel** into **The King's Gap**. Walk down to the **seafront**.

4. Turn left along the **beach** and follow the **sea wall** for a little over a kilometre to the low sandstone outcrop of **Hilbre Point** overlooking **Red Rocks**. (If the tide is very high, return to Stanley Road and walk down the road instead.)

5. Beyond the **slipway** at the end of **Stanley Road**, pick up a sandy path above a beach and then follow it as it joins a broad grassy path between sand dunes on the left and saltmarsh on the right. Follow the estuary path back to West Kirby, where you cross a beach and climb steps into **South Parade**.

6. Head along the **promenade** then turn right just before the **Sailing Centre** to join the **causeway around the Marine Lake** (at very high tides this may be flooded, in which case stay on South Parade). Follow the causeway for a little over a kilometre until it curves back to dry land at **West Kirby Sailing Club**. Beyond the sailing club join **Sandy Lane**, straight ahead.

7. Immediately after a **railway bridge**,

turn right into **York Avenue**, then right down steps onto the **Wirral Way**. Turn right under the bridge and follow the

Looking out across the sands from Hoylake to the Hilbre Islands

former railway for 400 metres to the next overbridge, before which you turn right up **steps**. Turn right at the road, and then right again into the churchyard of **St Bridget's Parish Church**. Pass to the right of the church tower to an exit in the far corner by **St Bridget's Primary School** and **West Kirby Museum**.

8. Turn left along **Church Walk** to return to **Church Street**. Turn right along **Rectory Road** then, when the road bends right, turn left onto a signposted public footpath (**Echo Lane**) which climbs between stone walls to **Village Road**. Cross straight over and climb the steps to **The Column**.

Turn left along a narrow path through gorse to a road junction. Beyond **Village Road**, cross **Column Road** opposite Majestic Wines. Turn left to cross **Black Horse Hill** and follow **Grange Old Road**, which bends to the left. Just before the main road, turn right onto a footpath at the entrance to **Grange Hill**. This metalled path winds below gardens, then turns left between gorse bushes to the **Hoylake and West Kirby War Memorial**.

9. Just past the memorial, turn left then right onto a narrow path that descends over **rock steps** in the direction of Hilbre Island in the distance, before bearing left to

the end of **Claremont Road**. Walk down the road to its junction with **Darmonds Green**, where you turn right. Turn left down **Bridge Road**, crossing **Orrysdale Road** and the **railway**, to return to **Grange Road** and the **West Kirby Tap**. Retrace your steps back to **Dee Lane** and **South Parade** to complete the walk. ♦

Red Rocks Nature Reserve

The saltmarsh and dune system around Hilbre Point is a Site of Special Scientific Interest (or SSSI) supporting specialised maritime plants such as sea holly and a variety of seabirds, including vocal summer flocks of Sandwich terns out on the sandy flats. The rare natterjack toad inhabits brackish pools between the dunes, from where its loud and rasping calls can sometimes be heard on spring evenings.

The Harp Inn overlooks the Dee Estuary's broad tidal marshes

Harp Inn
Little Neston

What to expect:
Surfaced rail trail, paved esplanade and estuarine path with boardwalks

Distance/time: 8 kilometres / 5 miles. Allow 2–3 hours

Start: Car park at Denhall Quay, adjacent to Harp Inn, Little Neston

Grid Ref: SJ 290 761

Ordnance Survey map: Explorer 266 *Wirral & Chester/Caer*

The Pub: Harp Inn, 19 Quayside, Little Neston CH64 0TB
0151 336 6980 | www.facebook.com/theharpinnneston

Walk outline: After a short stretch above the Dee saltmarsh, our route heads inland and picks up the Wirral Way, a former railway line. Returning to the shore, the route heads along Parkgate esplanade before returning to the atmospheric reedbeds and bird-filled skies of the estuarine marshes.

The Harp Inn once served the adjacent embarkation point of Denhall Quay, associated with Neston Colliery. It's still an unpretentious and unrestored local pub, but its setting could scarcely be improved; turning the corner from the housing estates that line its approach is like being suddenly transported from suburbia to a hidden corner of the Welsh coast.

The Harp Inn, Little Neston

▶ Harp Inn at a glance

Open: All day from 12 noon; food served until 3pm only, except for Tuesday curry nights
Brewery/company: Free house
Real ales: Three regular cask ales plus two guests
Food: Lunchtime only, including pub-grub mains, 'light bites', sandwiches, toasties and desserts
Accommodation: None
Outside: Picnic tables on the lawn overlooking the estuary
Children & dogs: Dogs welcome; children are permitted away from the bar area

The Walk

1. From the front of the **pub**, facing the estuary, turn right. When the road bends inland, continue along the path beside the estuary. After 600 metres, cross a stone stile by the walls of the **Old Quay**.

2. Turn right, away from the shore, and follow the obvious path through fields, crossing a **footbridge**, with a **treatment works** to your left. The path meets a hedged track and bears left; turn right almost immediately through a kissing gate and cross a field to a **former railway line**; carry on along the left-hand edge of the next field to a gate onto the **Wirral Way**.

3. Turn left and follow the combined cycle-path and bridleway for 500 metres to a **red-brick overbridge**, ignoring a crossing path about halfway. Continue along the **Wirral Way** for a similar distance beyond the bridge to **Station Road car park**. Descend the steps by the former **pillbox** to the road.

4. Cross into **The Ropewalk** opposite and turn right just beyond an **electricity substation** onto a **cobbled path** that curves back to the **Wirral Way**. Turn left and follow the former railway for another 500 metres to cross **Brooklands Road Bridge**. After a further 500 metres, pass under the **grey-brick overbridge** carrying **Boathouse Lane**.

5. Leave the **Wirral Way** via steps on the right just before **Backwood Hall Bridge**. Turn left over the bridge and follow the broad path down to the **estuary**.

6. Turn left and walk through the **Old Baths car park** to meet the road at the **Boathouse pub**. Stroll along **Parkgate esplanade** above the **sea wall** for a kilometre to the **Old Quay pub**, passing various pubs, cafés and shops.

The tumbled remains of Denhall Quay at Little Neston

7. Continue along the sea wall past the Old Quay pub and follow the path along the wall and then left between gardens. Turn right along a suburban road at a footpath sign to the end, and follow a path between barriers to another road. Continue along **Manorial Road South** until it bends left, where you leave it, turning right alongside the last house to return to the edge of the **estuary**.

8. Turn left along a narrow, reed-lined path. This path can be muddy in places and crosses a number of **footbridges** and **short boardwalks**. Eventually, beyond a **metal kissing gate**, you cross a couple of **footbridges** in some grassy paddocks to rejoin the outward path at the **Old Quay**. Retrace your steps along the edge of the saltmarshes back to the **Harp Inn** to complete the walk. ♦

Dee Marshes
Dredging of the Dee caused silting on the English side, leaving a wide band of saltmarsh that attracts wading birds. At exceptionally high tides, these low-lying areas are flooded once more, and rodents and small birds are forced into a narrow strip below the sea wall. This attracts raptors such as hen harriers, short-eared owls and barn owls, which in turn bring groups of birdwatchers and photographers flocking to the Old Baths at Parkgate.

The Ring o' Bells pub faces St Laurence's Church on Overton Hill

The Ring o' Bells
Frodsham

Distance/time: 5 kilometres / 3¼ miles. Allow 2 hours

Start: Large church car park opposite the pub

Grid Ref: SJ 521 772

Ordnance Survey map: Explorer 267 *Northwich & Delamere Forest*

The Pub: The Ring o' Bells, 2 Bellemonte Road, Frodsham WA6 6BS
|01928 732068 | www.ringobells-frodsham.co.uk

Walk outline: The outward path undulates gently along the bottom of the wooded slopes of Frodsham Hill before a short but stiff climb to the top. The high-level return is interrupted by the sharp ravine of Dunsdale Hollow before a climb-and-contour walk to a climactic viewpoint, followed by a straightforward descent.

The Ring o' Bells is a traditional white-painted pub housed in a Grade II listed building in a villagey position opposite the Norman church of St Laurence, with a comfortable beamed interior divided into small rooms with cosy fireplaces. There is also a flower-filled beer garden for warmer days.

Painted pub sign

▶ The Ring o' Bells at a glance

Open: From 10am for breakfasts until last orders at 11pm; food until 9pm
Brewery/company: J W Lees
Real ales: Four cask ales from the Lees stable
Food: All-day breakfasts from 10am onwards, plus a standard pub menu served till 9pm
Accommodation: None
Outside: Pleasant beer garden to rear, with tables
Children & dogs: Welcome throughout

The Walk

1. From the front door of the **pub**, turn left and cross to the **church**. Take the walled, surfaced footpath to the left of the churchyard wall between church and car park.

St Laurence's Church dates from around 1180 – the pillars and two of the arches between the aisles and nave date from this period. The clerestory windows, high in the walls above the arcades, are of similar date. Norman work is relatively rare in Cheshire churches.

At the end of the left-hand wall, turn left on a metalled path that crosses **Churchfields play area**. At the end of Churchfields go down the steps and look for a footpath on the left between gardens to reach **Howey Lane**. Cross the road and take broad path/access road almost opposite known as **Bottom Walk** (by a house called **Beechlands**).

2. Follow Bottom Walk round to the right and continue as it narrows to a **woodland bridleway** running along the backs of the gardens.

After about 500 metres of ignoring any turnings to left or right, you pass a row of houses on the left and follow the drive beyond to emerge at the top of **Carriage Drive**.

3. Turn left past an entrance marked 'Dunsdale' and follow the gently ascending bridleway beyond a wooden gate at the limit of traffic. At the end of the wall on your right, turn right down **stone steps** and follow the wall to the bottom of the slope. Swing left here through an open area at the bottom of the **Dunsdale valley**. Ignore a minor

The viewpoint and seat below Woodhouses hillfort

path off to the left. Instead, continue on the undulating path beyond along the bottom of the wood for a kilometre or so, with views to the right over the Mersey estuary, until you meet a fence at the end of a driveway.

4. Turn left here and immediately start climbing the steep wooded slope up through **Woodhouses Hill Wood**, via intermittent **wooden steps**. Further up, rough **stone steps** wind between sandstone outcrops until you finally reach the top of the hill, to the left of a metal kissing gate.

5. Turn left gratefully along a level wooded path that runs between two tiers of **sandstone crags**. Beyond an illustrated **interpretation panel**, the route is soon joined by the **Sandstone Trail** descending from your right. Continue past a **bench on a crag** — *with a fine outlook over Frodsham Marsh and its wind turbines to the Mersey* — shortly followed by another similar **viewpoint**. Still following the yellow Sandstone Trail waymarks, skirt the edge of **Frodsham Golf Course**. Just after the 10th tee, descend a mildly rocky section called

A broad panorama spreads out below Overton Hill

Abraham's Leap, to a signposted path junction below a small cave in the cliff to the right. If you are nimble, and unconcerned by hands-on scrambling with mild exposure, you can attempt **Jacob's Ladder**, the rocky climb starting immediately ahead, but the more sensible or sedentary walker will bypass the climb by turning right up the valley (signposted 'Sandstone Trail Frodsham') and then using the metal **Baker's Dozen steps** on the left instead.

The Sandstone Trail runs for 34 miles from Frodsham to Whitchurch in Shropshire, generally following the mid-Cheshire ridge.

6. Keep along the **Sandstone Trail**, ignoring a path across the golf course on the right but otherwise bearing right wherever there are choices while staying within the woodland. Eventually you pass just below the end of a **hotel complex** and, bearing right at a junction with a lower path, reach the open space surrounding **Frodsham War Memorial**, where there are further panoramic views.

7. Beyond the memorial, still keeping to the scarp, follow the narrow path with a white waymark to a **Sandstone Trail fingerpost** indicating 'Frodsham Centre'. Follow it, turning sharp left off the continuing path, and descend to a

flight of **wooden steps**. At the foot of the steps, turn right to descend to **Middle Walk**, a broad path along the contour.

8. At the bottom of the slope, turn right and leave the woods to join a metalled road. Continue out to **Bellemonte Road** and turn left. Pass the end of **Hillside Road** and the **Bulls Head** pub to reach **St Laurence's Church** and the **Ring o' Bells** to complete the walk. ♦

Mersey View

From Frodsham War Memorial the view extends over a landscape punctuated by industry, from the Welsh hills in the west, via the chimneys of Stanlow and Ince and the new wind turbines of Frodsham Marsh to the works at Weston Point and Rocksavage. Beyond the turbines and the Mersey estuary, Liverpool's Anglican cathedral is visible in the distance, and the River Weaver winds into view from your right to meet the Manchester Ship Canal.

The 18th-century George & Dragon sits at the heart of Great Budworth

George & Dragon
Great Budworth

What to expect:
*Level paths through
fields, alongside a canal,
a beside a lake*

Distance/time: 8 kilometres / 5 miles. Allow 2½ hours

Start: Marbury Country Park – pay and display car park

Grid Ref: SJ 651 763

Ordnance Survey map: Explorer 267 *Northwich & Delamere Forest*

The Pub: George and Dragon, High Street, Great Budworth, Northwich CW9 6HF | 01606 892650 | www.georgeanddragonat-greatbudworth.co.uk

Walk outline: Field paths lead to Great Budworth, "one of the best pieces of villagescape in the county", and the George and Dragon, and thence to the Lion Salt Works museum. A stretch of Trent & Mersey towpath leads back into Marbury Country Park and through woods to Budworth Mere.

The George and Dragon has an enviable position at the heart of the village, in a listed building overlooking the church and village stocks. Food is locally sourced and freshly prepared in-house.

Ornate fretwork pub sign

▶ George & Dragon at a glance

Open: 11.30am–11pm daily; food till 9.30pm (8.30pm on Sundays)
Brewery/company: J W Lees
Real ales: Three real ales including Great Budworth Bitter, brewed especially for the pub
Food: Well-presented starters, mains and desserts, plus a range of hot and cold sandwiches, and roasts on Sunday. A gluten-free menu is available
Accommodation: None
Outside: Outdoor tables beneath parasols overlook the village
Children & dogs: Children welcome; dogs in the front bar, though not on the furniture

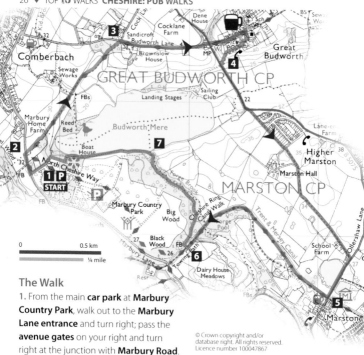

The Walk

1. From the main **car park** at **Marbury Country Park**, walk out to the **Marbury Lane entrance** and turn right; pass the **avenue gates** on your right and turn right at the junction with **Marbury Road**.

Marbury Country Park occupies the former grounds of Marbury Hall, a grand hall in the style of a French chateau, extensively remodelled by Antony Salvin of Peckforton Castle fame, but demolished in the 1960s. During the Second World War the house was the site of a German prisoner-of-war camp; Bert Trautmann, a German paratrooper who later famously kept goal for Manchester City, was held here.

2. Roughly 150 metres beyond **Marbury Hall Nurseries**, leave the road through a kissing gate with an **NCW (North Cheshire Way) waymark** on the right, into a field. Cross to a further kissing gate and follow the fence beyond, before dropping to a **footbridge** over **Kid Brook**. Climb to a further kissing gate and again follow the fence ahead, before bearing right across a field to a gate into

Great Budworth's pretty half-timbered houses and church

woodland. Follow the path through the wood up to **Budworth Lane**.

3. Turn right, ignoring the turning to **Budworth Heath**, and follow the road past some houses. Beyond the last driveway, continue along the now vergeless road. After a house the road drops sharply down to the **A559**, opposite the **covered well**. Cross and follow the road opposite, uphill and along the main village street of **Great Budworth** between cottages to the **George and Dragon**. From the pub, cross over past the **church** and **village stocks**. Turn right at the corner of the **churchyard** and then bear left past a house to a grassed area between hedges. Beyond a gate, follow the right-hand edge of a field down to the main road.

4. Turn left along the pavement for 450 metres, crossing a **stream** at the bottom of the valley. Cross to a **layby** on a left-hand bend and go through the kissing gate into a field. Follow the public footpath along the left-hand edge of two fields, uphill, then cross the drive to **Marston Hall** and continue along a footpath opposite. Beyond a kissing gate,

Ancient Budworth Mere is popular with anglers and boaters

continue across a field to a gate, beyond which you turn left and follow the hedge to a gate. Proceed past **School Farm** and out to the road. Turn right along the road, between **two subsidence meres**, to the **canal bridge** by the **Lion Salt Works** (entrance on left).

The Lion Salt Works operated from 1894 until closure in 1986 and interactive exhibits show how brine was evaporated in large iron salt pans. In 2016, the museum received a National Lottery award for Best Heritage Project, after a 30-year campaign to save what was the last open-pan saltworks in Britain and one of the last in the world. The site includes a café and children's play area.

5. Turn right and and double back to join the **towpath** of the **Trent & Mersey Canal**; turn left along the towpath, past a **former salt store**. Pass a sign reading "To the Pub" and continue along the towpath for almost a mile, following the canal as it bends westwards.

6. At a **footbridge**, leave the towpath and cross to the northern bank of the canal and into **Marbury Country Park**. Turn right through the trees and follow the main path as it swings left away from the canal, ignoring paths on the left into open fields. As you approach the lake, take a path on the right that drops down to **Forge Brook**, and swing left to follow

it upstream, with occasional shallow steps, until you reach its **outlet from Budworth Mere**.

7. Bear left along the **lakeside path**, passing the '**grotto**' on the left, and then

a small **inlet**. Shortly before you reach the boathouse, leave the lakeshore on a path to the left. Walk out past the park offices and covered picnic area back to the car park to complete the walk. ♦

Budworth Mere

Like many Cheshire lakes, Budworth Mere formed after subsidence of underlying salt deposits. Some such 'subsidence flashes' appeared only recently following commercial over-extraction of salt, but Budworth is natural and much older. Covering 80 acres, it is popular with anglers and yachtsmen. Notable birds include reed warblers, sedge warblers and great crested grebes, with occasional bitterns in winter.

The charming Boot Inn sits at the foot of hidden Boothsdale

The Boot Inn
Willington, near Kelsall

What to expect:
Fields and woodland on a sandstone scarp; one climb

Distance/time: 5 kilometres / 3 miles. Allow 2 hours

Start: Car park at Willington Corner

Grid Ref: SJ 530 667

Ordnance Survey map: Explorer 267 *Northwich & Delamere Forest*

The Pub: **The Boot Inn**, Boothsdale, Willington, near Tarporley CW6 0NH | 01829 751375 | www.thebootinnwillington.co.uk

Walk outline: Climb the mid-Cheshire ridge, with wide views over the Cheshire Plain, to the Sandstone Trail and the Urchin's Kitchen, within the shady depths of Primrose Wood. Fieldside paths with more views lead past an Iron Age hillfort, before a delightful descent through Boothsdale — a wooded combe known more romantically as 'Little Switzerland' — takes you down to the hidden Boot Inn.

The Boot Inn, occupying a charming row of former cottages, sits in splendid isolation at the end of a no-through road. Within its flower-hung walls you will find a cosy, traditional pub with a good local reputation for its food.

Tempting menu

▶ The Boot Inn at a glance

Open: Food available 11am–2.30pm and 6–9.30pm, or all day on Fridays, weekends and Bank Holidays
Brewery/company: Weetwood Brewery, Kelsall
Real ales: A selection of Weetwood Ales, plus a well-chosen wine list
Food: Satisfying mains and Sunday roasts alongside light meals, salads, sandwiches and baked potatoes for those with smaller appetites
Accommodation: None
Outside: Tables on the front terrace with more in the cottage garden
Children & dogs: Children welcome; dogs outside only

The Walk

1. From the car park by the small green at **Willington Corner**, walk away from the road junction up **Chapel Lane** to **Willington Fruit Farm**.

2. Keep right along the road, overlooking the deep valley of **Pearl Hole** on the right. *The retaining wall above the drop was built by German prisoners-of-war in 1946/7 as revealed by a faint inscription on one of its blocks.*

Continuing through open country, keep right at the junction with **Waste Lane** to a right-hand bend. Leave the road on the **Sandstone Trail**, signposted to the left beside a house and former tearoom.

Follow the right-hand field-edge beyond, before passing through a metal kissing gate and swinging left to reach a further kissing gate into **woodland**.

3. Turn left along the forest edge, passing a **Peak & Northern Footpaths Society signpost**. When you see a **mossy rock outcrop** in the field on your left, turn right, into the wood, following a **Sandstone Trail** waymark. At a crossing track, carry straight on, signposted to the 'Urchin's Kitchen'. Beyond the gorge, at the foot of the wood, turn left. After 100 metres, turn left again, back into the wood. Ignore a crossing footpath and return to the surfaced path.

4. Ignore the Sandstone Trail (which heads off to the right) and follow the track ahead and slightly to the right, which leads out to the road at **King's Gate**. Turn right and follow the road round a left-hand bend. Beyond a **pond**, when the road bends right, turn left into a drive that leads to a footpath along the bottom of a wood.

5. At the end of the wood go through a kissing gate and swing left across undulating open fields. To the right here are the faint, earthen banks of an ancient promontory fort called **Kelsborrow Castle.** *The fortifications belong to an Iron Age hillfort, one of only seven in Cheshire. To the south and west the site is*

0   0.5 km
½ mile

An elevated path runs down the flank of pretty Boothsdale

naturally defended by the steep slopes looking over Boothsdale, but an earthen rampart protected the northern and eastern approaches and can still be seen today, though much reduced by subsequent ploughing.

Beyond a kissing gate the path goes down some steps and swings right around the head of the valley known as **Little Switzerland**, before descending to meet a driveway and then a road.

6. Turn right here, down a tunnel-like hedged path to the **Boot Inn**.

To return to the **car park**, walk down the lane beyond the pub to a T-junction. Turn left and follow the road for 400 metres back to the start at **Willington Corner** to complete the walk. ♦

Urchin's Kitchen

The Urchin's Kitchen is a shallow, meandering sandstone gorge, about six metres deep, carved by glacial meltwater towards the end of the last Ice Age, when the retreating ice-sheet was held back by the Mid-Cheshire Ridge. Noting that the top of the gorge is narrower than the bottom, geologists suggest that the water that scoured it out it was under enormous pressure beneath the overlying ice-sheet.

The Pheasant Inn was a working dairy farm until the 1950s

The Pheasant Inn
Higher Burwardsley

What to expect:
Wooded hills and field paths

Distance/time: 8 kilometres / 5 miles. Allow 2–3 hours

Start: Sandstone Trail car park at the Cheshire Workshops, Higher Burwardsley

Grid Ref: SJ 522 564

Ordnance Survey map: Explorer 257 *Crewe & Nantwich*

The Pub: The Pheasant Inn, Higher Burwardsley, Tattenhall CH3 9PF
01829 770434 | www.thepheasantinn.co.uk

Walk outline: Our route crosses the Peckforton Hills and descends to the gatehouse of Peckforton Castle. A field path leads above Peckforton Mere to the village of Beeston, and follows narrow lanes to Beeston Castle. The return is along the Sandstone Trail, which follows field paths with views of both Peckforton and Beeston Castles before entering the woodland of the Peckforton Estate.

Housed in a former farmhouse and listed building, the upmarket Pheasant Inn has a terrace with superb views over the Cheshire Plain and the Welsh hills, and a large, secluded garden with parasol-shaded tables.

Stunning terrace views

▶ The Pheasant Inn at a glance

Open: 12 noon–11pm daily
Brewery/company: Nelson Hotel Group
Real ales: Real ales are from the local Weetwood Brewery and include Pheasant Gold, brewed exclusively for the pub
Food: British and European cuisine from local suppliers; includes hot and cold sandwiches and salads as well as the usual starters and mains
Accommodation: Twelve en-suite, dog-friendly rooms
Outside: Terrace with wide views, and a secluded garden to the side
Children & dogs: Welcome throughout

The Walk

1. From the **car park** entrance, turn left then immediately right into **Sarra Lane**, passing to the right of a brick house.

At the **crossroads**, go straight ahead into **Rock Lane**, marked as a no-through road. At a **fork**, keep right (up **Hill Lane**) past **Rock Farm**, and at a further junction between **two sandstone cottages**, carry straight on until the tarmac ends and the **Sandstone Trail** departs to the right.

2. Ignoring the Trail, carry on along the track ahead of you, passing a house on the left, to a **gate**. Continue along the track beyond, ignoring turnings to left and right, until you pass under a **stone bridge** carrying a private drive within the Peckforton Estate.

3. Shortly afterwards, beyond a **metal barrier**, leave the main track, turning left into a driveway and then immediately doubling back right past a footpath sign. The path bears left through trees to a stile into **open fields**. Descend to a further stile and then cross

a field diagonally to a kissing gate in the far corner, leading in short order to a **wooden step stile** and then **stone steps** in the wall down to the road.

Turn left and follow the road for a little over quarter of a mile to the **Peckforton Castle gatehouse**.

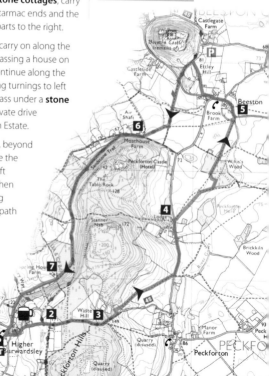

Beeston Castle is visible beyond a Tudor house on Horsley Lane

Peckforton Castle was built between 1844 and 1850 in the style of a medieval castle, by Anthony Salvin for John Tollemache, a wealthy Cheshire landowner and MP. It is now a hotel and wedding venue. The gatehouse is also by Salvin.

4. Just before the gatehouse, turn right through a stone squeeze stile and **kissing gate** to a footpath which skirts the right-hand side of a field, with glimpses of wooded **Peckforton Mere** to the right. Ignore a kissing gate on the right, instead skirting a wood ahead to a redundant stile, where the path turns right into **Willis's Wood**.

Emerging from the wood at a stile, continue ahead past a **pond** on the left and then strike out across the field beyond, aiming slightly right of the buildings at the far side. Negotiate a stile into a track in the corner and walk out to the road.

5. Turn left and follow the road past the half-timbered **Brook Farm Cottage** to **Beeston village**. Turn left at a T-junction (signposted to Beeston Castle) and then turn right in front of another half-timbered cottage, still following the **signs for Beeston Castle**.

Panoramic views from the top of Beeston Castle extend over eight counties

Walk past some 20th-century housing then turn right into **Chapel Lane**. Follow this narrow lane for quarter of a mile until you reach the **Sandstone Café**. For **Beeston Castle** turn right, otherwise turn left along the **Sandstone Trail**, passing behind the café onto a path alongside the **castle wall** into woodland. Bear left along the top edge of the wood before turning right and descending through the trees to emerge into **Tattenhall Lane**.

Turn left past **Tabernacle Cottage** then immediately right, **up steps to a kissing gate**, still following the **Sandstone Trail**. Cross a field, with views of Peckforton Castle ahead and Beeston Castle behind, to a **footbridge over a stream** and continue ahead after a few steps up. At a kissing gate, turn right and cross the field diagonally to another kissing gate into **Horsley Lane**.

6. Turn right past a series of houses on your right, then leave Horsley Lane at a metal gate onto a footpath into the woods on your left, following the **Sandstone Trail**. The path climbs gradually, with wooded slopes on your left and views to the right. Carry straight on at a **crossing above an isolated cottage**, then part ways with the Sandstone Trail when it leaves to

climb up through the woods on your left, instead continuing along the descending, sunken way to exit the Estate woodlands at a gate at the end of **Pennsylvania Lane**.

7. Follow the lane to the **Pheasant Inn**. To return to the car park, continue past the pub and go straight on into **Barracks Lane** to complete the walk. ♦

Beeston Castle

Unlike neighbouring Peckforton Castle, which is a Victorian imitation, Beeston Castle is a genuine medieval fortification. Built in the 1220s, it stands on a prominent sandstone crag and is in the care of English Heritage. Although slighted on Cromwell's orders after the Englsih Civil War in 1646, enough of the inner and outer baileys survive today to give a lasting impression of the castle's defensive attributes.

The Swan Inn at Marbury seen from the 'Waterloo Oak'

The Swan
Marbury

Distance/time: 5.5 kilometres / 3½ miles. Allow 2 hours

Start: The Swan, Marbury – parking by permission only, or try School Lane for street parking

Grid Ref: SJ 561 457

Ordnance Survey map: Explorer 257 *Crewe & Nantwich*

The Pub: The Swan, Wrenbury Road, Marbury, Whitchurch SY13 4LS | 01948 522860 | www.swanatmarbury.co.uk

What to expect:
Field paths with numerous stiles, a gradual climb and potential mud

Walk outline: Field paths and a quiet lane lead you to Wirswall Hill, from which there are superb views over the local meres to the Peckforton Hills and, more distantly, the Clwydian Hills to the west and the Peak District to the east. A pleasant descending return leads back past scenic Marbury Big Mere to the village.

The Swan is a handsome Victorian building in a village setting so traditional as to be almost a cliché, what with its half-timbered black-and-white cottages, 13th-century St Michael and All Angels' church, and venerable oak tree commemorating the Battle of Waterloo.

'The Swan' pub sign

▶ The Swan at a glance

Open: All day from 11.30am; food from noon till 9.30pm (9pm Sundays)
Brewery/company: Free house
Real ales: Ales from Weetwood and Stonehouse breweries, plus guests
Food: Original and traditional mains (smaller portions available), plus sandwiches and lighter meals. Vegetarian, gluten-free and vegan options
Accommodation: None
Outside: Large patio with parasols between pub and half-timbered barn
Children & dogs: Children welcome; dogs anywhere except the garden room

The Walk

The oak tree opposite the Swan Inn, encircled by a seat, is traditionally associated with the Battle of Waterloo, though it was actually planted a year or two before the battle took place. The smaller tree on the green was added in 1994 to celebrate the centenary of Marbury Parish Council. The Swan Inn has been in operation since at least 1765, but the current building dates from the 1880s. Its adjoining barn, however, is 17th-century and Grade II listed, as are the Black and White Cottages opposite.

1. From the pub's main entrance, turn right between **black-and white buildings** and continue past the turning to the **church** (left) and the car park entrance (right). At the junction of **Wirswall Road** and **School Lane**, turn left over a stile. Bear right to a further stile, and continue in the same direction to a third. Turn left along a concrete-sleepered track that crosses a series of **three bridges** over ditches. After the third, turn right to a stile beyond a **circular water trough**. Aim to the right of a solitary tree in the next field to a stile into **Wirswall Road**.

2. Turn left and follow the narrow lane for 800

metres, following the road round a right-hand bend as waymarked.

3. Turn left into a driveway at the 'Wirswall' sign, and climb a stile on the right. Curve rightwards across the field ahead to an initially hidden stile by a gateway. Climb the highest part of the next field to another gateway and then

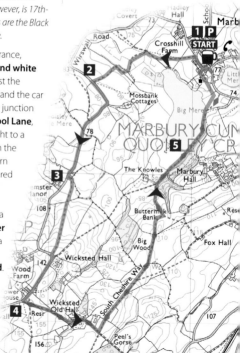

Looking down on Marbury Mere from Wirswall Hill

climb to the right-hand of two stiles at the top of the field.

The view from Wirswall Hill encompasses much of Cheshire. To the northwest the skyline is dominated by the Peckforton Hills — from left to right, Bickerton Hill, Raw Head, Bulkeley Hill, Stanner Nab and Beeston Castle — and in front of them the two Quoisley Meres. Turning clockwise, the church at Marbury overlooks Big Mere, and behind them you may be able to pick out the saltworks chimney at Middlewich and the radio telescope at Jodrell Bank. The hills of the Peak District, from the Roaches and Morridge in the south to Sutton Common,

Shutlingsloe and beyond further north, provide a distant backdrop to your right.

Having admired the view behind you, rejoin **Wirswall Road** and turn left, passing the two entrances to **Wicksted Hall**.

4. After 400 metres, at a right-hand bend, turn left into a **fenced driveway** with a public footpath sign. Follow the driveway to a T-junction, where you turn left to pass between **Wicksted Old Hall** and its **brick barns**.

Turn right at a **South Cheshire Way** ('SCW') waymark and continue straight

Looking across Marbury Big Mere to the church and village

ahead to a stile when the farm track bends left. Follow the fence to a four-way fingerpost, where you turn left (signposted 'Marbury') and climb to another stile, with impressive views. *The obelisk to your right is an 1890 memorial to Field Marshal Viscount Combermere within the grounds of Combermere Abbey.*

Walk along the broad ridge, keeping to the left of a wooded bank to a concealed stile by a gate. Head down the hill, looking for a stile in the left-hand hedge (ignore another in the bottom right-hand corner). Follow the field-edge beyond to a further stile, then follow a small dry valley downhill towards **The Knowles**,

an isolated house, before bearing right to the woodland edge and a gate and stile. Keep towards the right-hand side of the next field, boggy in places, until you reach another stile and gate in the corner, beyond which is **Marbury Mere**.

5. Follow the tree-shaded path ahead, with the lake on your left, to a stile into open fields. After a second stile, the public footpath heads right to a gate into the road, but an unofficial path bears left up the hill to a gate to the right of **St Michael's Church**.

The parish church of St Michael is in a wonderful position overlooking Big Mere. As at Wybunbury (see Walk 8) its

'Perpendicular' tower leans as the result of underground salt subsidence. Interesting features inside include a 15th-century pulpit and a funeral bier from the early 20th century. An external curiosity is that the only clockface on the tower is positioned to benefit the inhabitants of Marbury Hall, rather than the villagers.

Leave the churchyard via the lychgate and follow the lane round to the right, to emerge opposite the Swan car park to complete the walk. ♦

Marbury Big Mere

Marbury was recorded as Merberie *in the Domesday Book, indicating that the adjacent mere was already a defining feature of the village in 1086. An angler had a shock in 1998 when he fished part of a human skull from the waters of Big Mere: archeological assessment of the find, and other bones discovered during the subsequent police search, showed them to be Saxon in date.*

The Swan Inn at Wybunbury seen from the beer garden

Swan Inn
Wybunbury

What to expect:
Marshland boardwalks and rolling field paths

Distance/time: 7 kilometres / 4½ miles. Allow 2–3 hours

Start: Swan Inn, Wybunbury - pub car park by permission only, or plentiful nearby street parking

Grid Ref: SJ 699 498

Ordnance Survey map: Explorer 257 *Crewe & Nantwich*

The Pub: The Swan Inn, 2 Main Road, Wybunbury, Nantwich, Cheshire CW5 7NA | 01270 841280 | www.swaninn.pub

Walk outline: From the churchyard of the former church of St Chad (reduced by subsidence to just the tower) the route drops down a slope and joins a permitted path, partly on boardwalks, through the low-lying marsh and woodland of Wybunbury Moss, a National Nature Reserve. Field paths lead to Lea Hall, a substantial black-and-white Tudor house, before you pick your way through an area of disused and active sand pits back to Wybunbury village.

The Swan is a charming, rambling listed building in an enviable position next to Wybunbury Tower in the centre of the village.

Wybunbury's own ale

▶ The Swan Inn at a glance

Open: Daily, 12 noon–11pm
Brewery/company: Robinsons
Real ales: Real ales from the Robinsons stable
Food: Grills and homemade pies a speciality (vegetarian options), served all day at weekends and until 3pm and from 6pm during the week
Accommodation: Seven en suite rooms in stable block to rear
Outside: Tables out front, plus beer garden with views of Wybunbury Tower

The Walk

1. From the entrance to the **pub car park**, turn left by the **lych gate** and approach **Wybunbury Tower**.

Wybunbury Tower is all that remains of St Chad's Church. There have been at least five church buildings on this site, but the unstable salt-bearing strata beneath have led to repeated collapses and demolitions and left the tower with a pronounced lean. The first attempt at securing it in the 19th century pioneered techniques later used at the Leaning Tower of Pisa. Although it has now been straightened and secured using modern engineering, the tower has been deliberately left at a slight angle to maintain its status as the 'Leaning Tower of Cheshire'. Ironically, it is built in the Perpendicular style of Gothic architecture.

Beside an **information panel** on the left, a path constructed from old gravestones leads down to a kissing gate beside what appears to be a **medieval cross shaft**. Pass to the right of an **information panel** for Wybunbury Moss and walk down the slope to join a farm track that passes between a **stream** and a **pond**, both clogged with reeds. Beyond a

0   1 km
½ mile

farm gate and **bridge**, swing left on a permitted path to a **footbridge** and kissing gate into the **nature reserve**.

2. **Boardwalks** and **footbridges** lead past a further stile to a padlocked gate at the end of the open part of the moss. Turn right over a **footbridge** and right again, on a narrow path alongside a ditch that then bends left into **woodland**.

Wybunbury Tower and lychgate viewed from the Swan Inn

Follow the narrow path over **more boardwalks and footbridges** to a **footbridge** and a gate into open fields. More **boardwalks** lead across wet meadows to a gate in a hedge and thence to a kissing gate onto the public footpath at the edge of the reserve.

3. Turn right along a tree-lined path to a kissing gate into open fields, then turn left to a stile in the wooden fence. Walk up the slope to another stile into an area of hard-standing, where you bear half-right to another stile into paddocks. Cross a series of paddocks separated by stiles to a final stile at the top of the hill. Walk past a **linear pond** and then cross the field ahead to a kissing gate at the corner of a wood. Ignoring the gate, turn right along the bottom of the wood to another kissing gate, and continue along the field edge. The path swings 90° left by **Dove House Farm**; before the next kissing gate, turn right through another kissing gate and follow the hedge out to a kissing gate and into a road.

4. Cross the road and take a path to the left of the house opposite, which leads to a stile into fields. Follow the left-hand

Wybunbury Tower looms above the trees on the far side of Wybunbury Moss

edge until the hedge turns left, at which point you strike out across the field, passing to the left of a **dried-up pond**. Cross the driveway to **Ellesmere Farm** (with stiles waymarked 'SCW' for the South Cheshire Way) and walk down the hedge opposite, crossing a further stile, to the bottom of a valley. In the bottom corner of the field, turn right over a stile. Shortly, turn left over another stile by a farm gate and walk up the slope. Head for a metal gate giving access to the road. Turn left.

5. At the entrance to **Lea Hall**, turn right along a gravelly driveway. When this divides into three, take the track on the right (technically, the path skirts the field on the right). Beyond a kissing gate continue to the left of a hedge, descending and then climbing again. In the far corner, a stile leads down to a **green lane**, where you turn left through a gate and past a mobile mast. Follow the rough road ahead to **Lea Forge**.

6. Turn right onto an ascending quarry track, after a short while accompanied by a parallel footpath to the left (note: this path has recently been diverted and the exact line may vary depending on quarrying activities). Beyond the **quarry** the path descends to a **stream**, then curves left to a gateway into a field.

Bear right along the field edge with glimpses of a flooded quarry on your right. At the end of the field in the corner is a stile into a paddock, then a second stile to a path out to the road.

7. Turn left and follow the road for 500 metres back to **Wybunbury**. At a T-junction, turn right past the **Red Lion** to return to the **Swan** to complete the walk. ♦

Wybunbury Moss

Wybunbury Moss is a National Nature Reserve, the highest designation for natural protection. The main point of interest is a schwingmoor, a rare habitat where an open lake has gradually become covered by a floating mass of sphagnum moss. The fragile surface is dangerous, but the permitted path sticks to boardwalks. The Moss is home to almost the entire British population of the rare ten-spotted pot beetle, as well as bog-loving plants like the round-leaved sundew.

The thatched and half-timbered White Lion at Barthomley was built in 1614

White Lion Inn
Barthomley

What to expect:
Mostly level field paths with numerous stiles

Distance/time: 9.5 kilometres / 6 miles. Allow 3 hours

Start: Church/village hall car park at Barthomley village, close to the White Lion, or some roadside parking beyond the pub

Grid Ref: SJ 767 524

Ordnance Survey map: Explorer 257 *Crewe & Nantwich*

The Pub: White Lion Inn, Audley Road, Barthomley, Crewe, Cheshire CW2 5PG | 01270 882242 | www.whitelion-barthomley.co.uk

Walk outline: A footpath leads across rolling fields and over the Staffordshire boundary to the Tudor mansion of Hall o'th' Wood. More farmland walking brings you back into Cheshire and the pretty hamlet of Englesea Brook, with its early Methodist chapel and museum. From there, paths and quiet lanes lead back to Barthomley.

The White Lion Inn is worth a visit in its own right. Grade II* listed and dated 1614, it is included in CAMRA's National Inventory of Historic Pub Interiors and was voted their Unspoilt Pub of the Year for 2016. A section of original wattle and daub can be seen exposed in the bar.

Traditional painted sign

▶ White Lion Inn at a glance

Open: All day from 12 noon; food served lunchtimes only (to 2pm Mondays and Tuesdays, 3pm the rest of the week)
Brewery/company: Marstons
Real ales: Six cask ales from Marstons plus Jennings, Thwaites and Banks
Food: Chalkboard menu contains mostly pub-grub staples, plus sandwiches and desserts, including ice creams
Accommodation: None
Outside: Picnic tables on the cobbled area out front
Children & dogs: Dogs welcome on leads; children away from bar area

The Walk

1. Climb to the **churchyard**, exiting in front of the **tower**. Turn left past the **village hall** into a wooded path right of a **pond**, to a stile into fields. Turn left over another and strike out across the field with a **pond** on your left. At the far side, aim right of a gateway to a stile in a gap. Cross to another stile (initially hidden) and continue to a third at the projecting corner of the next field. Follow the field edge to yet another stile at the top of some **steps**. Bear right to another stile with a **Two Saints Way disk**. Climb the slope obliquely and proceed to a stile into woodland. Bear right to emerge in **Mill Dale** by a **pond**.

2. Turn left to a double gate, continuing along a wooded bank then dropping to the valley bottom by another **pond**. Turn left, past a **bridge at the top of the lake**, and continue through a gateway to a house. Turn right through the gate across a parking area to a **footbridge**, then climb steeply to a stile.

Bear left then swing right across the field, following the telegraph poles to a stile. Walk partway across the next field, then turn right to a concealed stile in the right-hand boundary. Aim towards **Shortfields**, in the far right-hand corner of the next field, and cross the drive and two stiles. Step out across the field ahead to an ornate double kissing gate by the gates of **Hall o' th' Wood**.

3. Follow the driveway past a **lake** then between

Englesea Brook chapel was founded by Primitive Methodists in 1828

the hall (left) and a **creeper-hung building** (right), passing a **pair of gate-piers** in the wall on your left. Swing left past a **garage**, then right and immediately left through a waymarked gate. Pass a **greenhouse** and climb a stile into fields. Follow the left-hand edge to a gate. Follow the track ahead (ignoring a turning to the right) past a house on the left to a metalled lane leading out to **Deans Lane**.

Turn right for 150 metres to a crossing footpath; turn left down a narrow footpath between gardens with a stile at each end.

Skirt a paddock to a third stile and cross a field to a fourth. Bear right to a projecting corner and follow the field edge to a fifth stile. Head half-right to a sixth stile, and cross the field beyond to a seventh stile (and **footbridge**) in a line of trees. Cross the last field to reach **Englesea Brook Lane**.

4. Cross and follow a gravelled path left of a bungalow. Beyond a stile, walk down to a **footbridge** at the valley bottom, continuing to a **second footbridge**. Climb the hill to a stile in the top left-hand

Traditional black and white cottages surround the old White Lion Inn

corner. Turn right and follow the driveway down to the road. Turn right down the lane to a junction. Divert to the right (recommended) to visit the **Chapel and Museum**.

5. Return to the bottom of **Snape Lane** and follow the road towards Barthomley, passing **Manor Farm**. After 500 metres, turn left over a stile by a gate. Head half-right to a stile in the wooden fence beside the driveway to **Town House Farm** and continue in the same direction to the far right-hand corner of the field, right of the farm.

A stile gives access to a short, narrow path to a further stile. Turn left to a double stile and, beyond, drop down a steep bank and cross to a **footbridge**. Cross a further field, looking out for a path into **scrubby woodland** on the left. After a stile you emerge at a field corner. Turn left then curve right to a waymarked stile into the busy **A500**.

6. Cross and take a signposted path opposite, to a stile overlooking a deep **flooded hollow**. Turn right up the bank and walk parallel to the road, before bearing left down a steep bank to a **farm bridge**. Turn right towards the main road again to the left-hand of two stiles in the corner. Follow the path above the A500 to a road.

7. Turn right over the **bridge**, then right onto a track between two **white-painted cottages**. Drop to a **stream** and turn left up a track. When this ends, follow the field edge ahead to a stile by a **pond**. Cross to a stile into a **green lane** and turn left.

8. At the road, turn right to a triangular junction. Follow the road signposted to 'Barthomley' and back to the **White Lion** to complete the walk. ♦

Primitive Methodism

Methodism began when followers of John Wesley, who preached initially in private houses and in the open air, split from the Church of England. The Primitive Methodists in turn broke from the Wesleyans following an open-air revival meeting at Mow Cop in 1807, and Englesea Brook (1828) was one of their earliest chapels. Hugh Bourne, a co-founder of the movement, is buried in the chapel's small graveyard.

THE SHIP

THE SHIP INN

Flowers and rustic benches outside the Ship Inn at Wincle

The Ship Inn
Wincle

What to expect:
Hill and woodland with stiles; some rocky paths

Distance/time: 8 kilometres / 5 miles. Allow 3 hours

Start: Roadside parking downhill from the Ship Inn, near the brewery entrance

Grid ref: SJ 964 652

Ordnance Survey Map: Explorer 268 *Wilmslow, Macclesfield & Congleton*

The Pub: The Ship Inn, Barlow Hill, Wincle, Cheshire SK11 0QE | 01260 227217 | www.theshipinnwincle.co.uk

Walk outline: Climb to a prominent rock with fine views, then contour through woodland to the legendary Lud's Church. Having explored this dramatic chasm, our path descends to the pretty River Dane, which it follows downstream back to the Ship Inn.

The Ship Inn is a pretty stone-built public house in an attractive position above the River Dane, within the Peak District National Park and close to the Staffordshire border. Dog- and child-friendly, it is the starting point for many a walker. The pub name honours Sir Philip Brocklehurst, born at nearby Swythamley House, who accompanied Ernest Shackleton to the Antarctic. The expedition ship, the Nimrod, features on the inn sign.

In we go!

▶ The Ship Inn at a glance

Open: All day from noon; food served lunchtimes and evenings only during the week, all day at weekends (till 6pm on Sundays)

Brewery/company: J W Lees

Real ales: Four cask ales

Food: Freshly prepared mains and desserts, plus soups and sandwiches

Accommodation: None

Outside: Picnic tables in garden above car park

Children & dogs: Children and dogs welcome (the latter are excluded from carpeted areas)

The Walk

1. Cross the **bridge** over the **River Dane** and follow the road uphill to the **Methodist Chapel**, opposite which take a path (signposted to Back Forest and Gradbach) between **two cottages**. Cross a driveway and continue to a gate into a field, which you cross to a stile into **woodland**.

2. Wind through the trees before meeting another path, where you bear right to a **footbridge**. Climb the **rough steps** beyond, eventually reaching a stile at the end of the wood. Bear left across the field past an **isolated stone** to a stile. Turn right for a few steps toward the

farm then bear left, obliquely up the hill, to a stile in the corner. Turn right along the track for 250 metres to a **cattle grid**, beyond which turn left over a stile and up to a gate. Bear left up the hillside to the prominent **Hanging Stone**.

3. Climb the **steps** to the left of the rock to the top of the hill and bear right along a waymarked concessionary path, crossing a stile and continuing to the left of a **boggy pond** to a wall stile into a well-worn path. Turn left and keep straight on at a path junction, along the path signposted to 'Gradbach and Lud's Church'. This path follows a wall then

Steps lead out of the gritstone chasm of Lud's Church

crosses the **moor** to the top of a wood before reaching a junction of paths at **Castle Cliff Rocks**, a prominent rocky tor. Take the right-hand path, signposted to 'Lud's Church'.

4. After a short distance, turn right and descend into the rocky chasm of **Lud's Church**. The path passes between high cliffs and then divides, where you take the right-hand turn and shortly scramble up out of the right-hand side of the ravine. Bear left to the far end of the ravine and then (ignoring the obvious path ahead) turn left, passing a second

narrow exit from **Lud's Church** on your left and descending to an obvious path. Turn left and walk back to the path junction by **Castle Cliff Rocks**, passing the **lower entrance of Lud's Church** again on your way.

5. Turn right, signposted to 'Gradbach', and descend an obvious path through the trees. Shortly before reaching the valley bottom, turn left (signposted 'Gradbach') down some **rough stone steps** and then left (signposted 'Danebridge'). This path climbs, then bears right (again signposted to

Wincle Brewery sits on the banks of the River Dane near the Grade II listed bridge

Danebridge) and follows roughly parallel to the **river** for a kilometre.

6. On exiting the woods, the path climbs to a stile and over a shoulder of land before descending to pass behind **Back Forest Farm**. The path continues ahead through stiles and gates and above a **series of gullies**, before following a grassy trod above a gorsy slope to join the driveway to another farmhouse, **Back Dane**. When the drive swings right into the property, the path continues ahead, following a retaining wall to a stile into woodland.

7. After an **old gateway** within the wood,

keep right at a vague fork; the path rises and falls, with some short boardwalks, before descending to the bottom of the wood. After a **stepped boardwalk**, go through a gate on your right into fields and bear left down the slope.

Follow a narrow **riverside field** to a gate into a short **woodland track**, which leads out to the road (ignore a stile and steps on the left). On reaching the road, turn right over the **Dane bridge** and head back up to the **Ship Inn** to complete the walk. ♦

The River Dane rises high on the moors of the Peak District, passes Three Shires Heads

(where the counties of Derbyshire, Cheshire and Staffordshire meet) and eventually flows into the River Weaver, and thence the Mersey and the Irish Sea. An oddity is that some of its waters are diverted into a canal feeder not far below Danebridge, and channelled via Rudyard Reservoir to the Caldon Canal, whose waters end up in the Trent and ultimately enter the North Sea via the Humber, on the opposite coast.

Gawain and the Green Knight

In Sir Gawain and the Green Knight, an epic Arthurian poem surviving from the late 14th century, Gawain, one of the Knights of the Round Table, beheads the mysterious Green Knight when he appears at Camelot, but the green-clad figure picks up its own severed head and challenges Gawain to a second meeting at the Green Chapel. Lud's Church is the most commonly cited location of this fateful meeting.

Useful Information

Visit Cheshire
Cheshire's official tourism website, with sightseeing ideas, accommodation suggestions and event listings. www.visitcheshire.com

Sandstone Trail
Information on Cheshire's premier long-distance path: www.sandstonetrail.co.uk

Tourist Information Centres

Chester 01244 405 340 | welcome@chestervic.co.uk

Congleton 01260 271 095 | congletontic@cheshireeast.gov.uk

Macclesfield 01625 378 123 | macclesfieldtic@cheshireeast.gov.uk

Nantwich 01270 628 633 | tourist.information@nantwichtowncouncil.gov.uk

Cheshire breweries and pubs

The largest traditional brewery within the historic boundary of Cheshire is, by some distance, Robinsons, based in Stockport and with outlets across Cheshire and the northwest. Some of the Manchester brewers, such as J W Lees, also extend into Cheshire.

Among the new generation of microbreweries thriving within the county are Weetwood at Kelsall, the Bollington Brewing Company, the Beartown Beer Company in Congleton, and Spitting Feathers in Chester itself.

The websites of Cheshire's five CAMRA branches — South Cheshire, Macclesfield & East Cheshire, North Cheshire, Trafford & Hulme, and Chester & South Clwyd — are probably the first port of call for real ale enthusiasts. The branches come together each year to organise a Cheshire Beer Festival, normally held at Chester Racecourse in March. It's now rare to find a pub without a choice of hand-pulled ales.

Weather
The Met Office operates a 24-hour online weather forecast for Cheshire. See www.metoffice.gov.uk